Evaluating Website Content

by
Ellen Chamberlain

ISBN 0-87367-692-0

Bloomington, Indiana

This fastback is sponsored by the
Tokyo Japan Chapter of
Phi Delta Kappa International,
which made a generous contribution
toward publication costs.

Table of Contents

Introduction

Today, we enjoy distinct advantages over earlier generations in our search for knowledge. Online catalogs, full-text databases, and digitized books and manuscripts, connected to high-speed document delivery systems, have opened up unique and rare collections that used to be hidden in libraries, museums, and private collections around the world. In many cases, these are works that in the past would have remained inaccessible to researchers, with the exception of those few who were able to visit the sites in person.

There is no doubt that seeking and finding information has become, through the years, an easier task. And yet, in some ways, it also has become more difficult due to the increasing number of information sources from which to choose. On the Internet, you soon learn that electronic information is not the same as print information found in bookstores and libraries. The difference derives from the absence of screening and filtering routinely carried out by editors, publishers, peers, booksellers, and librarians.

On the Internet, anyone can become his or her own publisher at very little individual expense. All it takes is a "host" to provide server space and a URL (Web address). The Web is democracy in action; and it can be, and often is, disorganized and messy.

The Internet has been called an "electronic library." However, it bears scant resemblance to the traditional libraries we know so well. For starters, the "electronic library" has no comprehensive card catalog, no professional staff members on duty, and no procedures in place to screen acquisitions. Its virtual shelves are as likely to hold political tracts, advertising, conversations, cheap tabloids, pornography, hoaxes, and deliberate frauds as they are to have rational and serious works from reputable sources. All of its holdings are mixed together in no apparent order, and none of them are labeled. Most important, in the electronic library, there is no bibliographic control, that is, no way to freeze a webpage in time. Because of the dynamic nature and constant evolution of the Web, the page you cite today may be altered or revised tomorrow, or it might disappear completely. The page owner may or may not acknowledge any changes to the text and, if he relocates the page, he may or may not leave a forwarding address.

With all of these obvious negatives, why would anyone choose electronic formats over print? Wouldn't it be better to avoid the freely available digital information altogether? The answer is that, if we avoid the Internet, we would miss too much that is valuable. Instead, we need to train ourselves to look at online information with a critical eye. We need to take the responsibility to evaluate and screen what we find.

This fastback will help users evaluate information on the Internet, specifically information that is freely avail-

author Kurt Vonnegut at MIT. Within days, the column had been forwarded to email addresses around the world. It still is available on the Web and, in many cases, still is attributed to Vonnegut (Schmich 1997).

While you cannot always discern the author's purpose, it's important to try. In a serious paper, to unknowingly include references to webpages that turn out to be advertisements, spoofs, or frauds is embarrassing and dilutes the credibility of the entire work.

Watch for these red flags:

- Apparent bias in the text.
- A suspicion you are being manipulated.
- Incomplete or one-sided presentation.
- Distorted facts or exaggerated opinions.
- Tone of voice at odds with subject matter.

Authority

Authority refers to the individual responsible for the content on the page. In a high-quality webpage, the name of the author is clearly stated in a prominent place. If the author has an affiliation with an organization, it is noted.

Unlike scholarly books and journal articles, websites seldom are reviewed or refereed and normally do not contain introductory or author notes that would provide credentials. Therefore, if an author's name appears on a page, it should be followed by additional information, such as credentials or experience, that clearly support the content and are verifiable.

The author also should supply a means for you to contact him, either through surface mail or an e-mail address. This does not always happen. E-mail addresses are easily falsified, as are credentials and statements of experience. Check both links and e-mail addresses to make sure they lead to authorized sources. If this is a content-packed page, the e-mail address of a webmaster, who is not the author, will not suffice; nor will addresses that turn out to be e-mail accounts freely available through commercial vendors and portals.

Of course, every individual who authors a webpage doesn't have to be a noted professional or a certified expert. He should not be averse, however, to telling you who he is and how he came by his knowledge. If what he says is legitimate, you will be able to verify it on other similar pages.

Verification of authority is especially important when the author lists no connection to any sponsoring body. Approach these pages with caution. They are most likely personal pages, created by individuals and hosted on the Web by an Internet service provider (ISP) for a monthly fee. The information they contain should be checked with other credible sources before you accept and use it.

Some pages do not list any individual's name as author of the textual material. In these cases, it is the sponsors — usually institutions, agencies, or business entities — that assume responsibility for the content. If they are well known to the public, they will have an established reputation on which you should be able to rely. If no sponsoring agency is listed or the name given is unknown to you, you'll need to look further to verify their authority.

One way to check authority is to see who is linking to the page from external sites, as well as what links are maintained by the page to other external sites. The links may be able to tell you a lot about the perceived quality of the page itself. Do the links connect to substantive sites that corroborate or add to the information you already accessed? Some search engines, such as Google, prioritize their retrieval lists based on link popularity: the more sites that point to a particular page, the higher that page's position is in Google's relevance rankings.

A page that lacks verifiable authority, either an individual author or a sponsoring agency, should be approached with skepticism. A few years ago, the *New Yorker* published a cartoon by Peter Steiner showing two dogs in front of a computer, with the one at the keyboard saying to the other, "On the Internet, nobody knows you're a dog." How true!

Watch for these red flags:

- Anonymous page author.
- Anonymous page sponsor.
- Inflated credentials (for example, title, education, experience, training) that lack authenticity.
- No credentials listed for author.
- Generic e-mail address for author that does not confirm authority claims.
- No provision for contacting author, through surface mail or e-mail, or by telephone or fax.

Currency

Currency refers to timeliness. It is reflected in the actual currency of the textual content and in the calendar updates noted on the bottom of the webpage. Checking the currency of webpages is important, though it is far from an exact science. No two sites approach currency in the same way. Some pages use dates to show the last time the links were checked. Others indicate the last time content was updated, while a few refer to the first time the page files were uploaded to the server. Then there are those that post no dates at all.

Of course, the more information that is provided, the more accurately you will be able to determine the currency of the page. However, even when dates are included, they can be ambiguous. A recent update may not ensure that the textual content is current but only that something on the page has been changed, for example, a misspelled word corrected or a typographical error fixed.

When it comes to the overall subject of currency, the Internet has a decided advantage over the world of print. This is mainly because electronic information can be created, updated, and disseminated in a matter of minutes, without having to wait for the next edition to appear days, months, or even years later. Currency becomes a very important factor when dealing with information in areas of rapid change, for example, when posting stock market quotations or late-breaking news. In fact, if you are unable to verify exactly when and how often pages such as these are updated, you had better not consult them.

Currency also is important when presenting information in the sciences, computer technologies, business, education, and the medical professions. All of these subjects depend on frequent updates and current news. On the other hand, the immediate availability of current information in the humanities (for example, literary criticism or historical analysis) may be less important.

Currency is one way to ascertain whether a page is continuing to be maintained. If there are numerous dead links, broken links, or empty files on a page, you may assume that it is unstable and would not be a reliable source. Page stability is especially important when you are writing a paper and using the Web for source material. Because websites are volatile and may be edited, moved, or deleted at any time, you need to pay close attention to the last update, as well as to the credentials and reputation of the page sponsor and author.

Always be sure to make and keep a backup copy (in print or on disk) of what you find on the Web. And be sure to record the date on which you found it. In this way, you will be able to verify your sources later on.

Currency on the Web cannot be taken for granted. You will find some pages unstable, changing without warning. Others that should be continuously updating their content may not change at all.

Watch for these red flags:

- No indication of last content update.
- No indication of last link update.
- Dates on page not current.
- Dead and broken links on page.

Content

Content refers to text. The content of a webpage may consist of both primary and secondary textual material.

Briefly, primary material is original information (manuscripts and documents), while secondary material is information about information (reviews and commentaries). Both kinds of content may contain facts, opinions, advice, and arguments. These elements are not always easy to separate.

Since anyone can publish anything on the Web, you should not be surprised to find more personal opinion than fact. Also, be aware that many Web authors are adept at convincing you that their opinions are facts. However, facts can be verified. They can be demonstrated, observed, or confirmed by reputable sources. Opinions are harder to quantify. They may be based on sound logic, experience, or research or they may have been plucked from thin air.

Whatever the nature of the content, you will want to know where the author got his information. Does he help you verify the subject by providing links to source materials that support the text? If he cites statistics, does he point you to reliable sources?

Content involves many elements of language, including style, coherence, and correctness. Examine the text. Is it explicit and precise? Look for clarity of expression and usage that is suitable to the content of the page. Be alert to vagueness in writing style, the frequent use of sweeping generalizations, stereotyping, or an overriding concern with ethnicity. These are not good indicators of quality content. Serious works do not depend on emotional rhetoric or fuzzy logic. The style they use is professional, concrete, and direct. Look for proper grammar and spelling. Whether from ignorance or carelessness, textual errors say something about the writer, and it's usually not positive.

Be sure to look at how well the page covers your topic. If you intend to cite this information in a paper, you will want a page that consists of more than just a series of links to other pages (unless it's a bibliography). The page should be one that covers your topic to the expected degree of depth and breadth and at a level appropriate for your needs.

Finally, try to distinguish between serious content and promotion or advertising. This is getting harder to do, as more pages seek to cover expenses by incorporating commercial advertisements into their subject matter. Use your common sense. Is the page truly informational, or is it actually an advertisement masquerading as information? What would you think if you knew that the favorable Web review of the new textbook you were about to purchase was written by the publisher? Always approach Web content with a critical eye.

Watch for these red flags:

- Unsupported claims or claims too good to be true.
- Apparent bias in the text.
- Coverage that appears skimpy or slight.
- Pages that consist primarily of links to other pages.
- Obvious textual inaccuracies, bad grammar, or misspelled words.
- Emotional rhetoric.
- Absence of links to other sites for corroboration or further information.

Page Design

Page design refers to appearance and workability. Good design is essential to information retrieval on the Web. Without it, serious seekers may not stay around long enough to discover what the page has to offer.

As members of a consumer society raised in an advertising age, we ought to be pretty familiar with design methods and media. However, the Web continues to open up new and innovative avenues in the field of audio and visual design. Website developers have become adept at creating attention-getting pages out of a mixture of graphic art, hot links, image maps, forms, cgi-scripts, audio and visual clips, Java Scripts, and Java applets. Many of these innovations assist in the acquisition of information, while others, such as popup ads, flashing banners, and an overabundance of animated gifs (images), are downright annoying.

Commercial sites, now the fastest growing category of sites on the Web, are clearly the most adept at using layout and design elements. As with every innovation, however, some of them tend to go overboard, allowing "glitzy" graphics or multiple, slow-loading images to take complete control of their pages.

The best designs maintain a reasonable balance between image and text and do not require visitors to traverse several layers of pages before finally reaching the textual content. Good designs avoid jarring color schemes and busy, cluttered layouts. They make good use of white space, fonts, and type sizes to assist the user in reading the screens.

Well-designed websites ensure a fast response time and provide text-only options and other alternatives for users with special needs. They do not require special helper applications, plug-in software extensions, or the latest browser releases to view their pages. They usually mount an internal search engine on the home page so that users may search the entire site.

Well-designed websites also create internal and external directional pointers to help users find their way around. They provide clear, easy-to-navigate pathways connecting each of the content pages to every other page and back to the home page. This is an important feature because search engines and other hyperlinks often drop users down into the middle of websites, rather than at their home pages, where most site-based navigational tools are found. Without access to at least one of these directional tools (a table of contents, site map, search engine, etc.), it is difficult to figure out where you are, much less where you might wish to go next. When a site migrates to a new server, well-designed websites create external pointers to the new location.

Good page designs attract viewers and enhance the usefulness of websites. Poor designs turn potentially useful pages into sites that are virtually inaccessible to the general public.

Watch for these red flags:

- No balance between image and text.
- Inadequate or missing navigational links within website.
- Too many large images that load slowly.

- No allowances for variations in computers and levels of connectivity.
- Page organization that hinders searching.
- Cluttered, difficult-to-read screens.

Using Web Addresses for Evaluation

Information on the Web comes in a variety of forms. Not all websites have the same look, feel, or substance. Some are more reliable than others are. For example, the most consistently trustworthy sites on the Web traditionally have been those sponsored by major universities, research centers, and government agencies, all of which put their names and reputations behind their pages. The least trustworthy sites are those authored by individuals, without credentials, who have no connection to any known organization.

Obviously, it is important to determine webpage sponsorship up front, but how do you do that when the information is not readily available on the sites themselves? One way is to extract it from the Web addresses, or URLs.

Web Addresses

The URL, which stands for Universal (or Uniforr Resource Locator, is the webpage address that app in the address box at the top of each visited ey Knowing how to read URLs is important becar Fo can tell you a lot about the page you are vie example, here is the URL for Bare Bones, a search engine tutorial I created in January 2000:

http://www.sc.edu/beaufort/library/bones.html

This is what it means when you break it down, reading from left to right:

Protocol://server.domain/directory/sub-directory/filename.filetype

- "http" is the transfer protocol (type of information being transferred).
- "www" is the host computer name (or server name).
- "sc" (University of South Carolina) is the second-level domain name.
- "edu" is the top-level domain name.
- "beaufort" is the directory name.
- "library" is the sub-directory name.
- "bones" is the file name.
- "html" is the file type and, in this case, stands for hypertext mark-up language.

For the purpose of evaluating content, the most important part of the URL is the top-level domain name, which identifies the type of sponsor. Only a few top-level domains currently are recognized, but this is hanging. The following is a list of the top-level domains ablished by Network Solutions, Inc., which pio- d in the development of registering Web addresses nain name:

.e

univer ducational sites, sponsored by colleges and s. These sites may contain pages created by faculty and students, as well as "official" pages created and maintained by administrative offices within the institutions. Outside the United States, academic sites are identified by use of the "**.ac**" domain. Sites in the .edu and .ac domains are considered very reliable.

.com: commercial sites, sponsored by business interests. Commercial sites are the most numerous sites on the Web and the fastest growing as well. They include large and small businesses, commercial enterprises, individual entrepreneurs, and news media and entertainment outlets. They should be approached with caution because, while they are good information sources, the information they provide is usually one-sided.

.gov: U.S. government sites, sponsored by branches, agencies, and departments of the U.S. government. These are non-military sites. They are a good source for primary documents and current statistics and are considered very reliable.

.mil: U. S. military sites, sponsored by branches of the military. Many of these sites are similar to the ".com" sites in that they have their own agenda. Approach them with caution.

.net: networks, sponsored by Internet service providers, telecommunications companies, and networking organizations. This category includes commercial sites as well as personal pages that are authored by individuals who pay a monthly fee for the server space. These pages are not screened, so you should be cautious in their use.

.org: U.S. professional and nonprofit organizations and others, sponsored by a variety of sources, including individuals. This category is home to many "advocacy" sites that are openly one-sided and created to influence public opinion. Approach these pages with cautious skepticism.

An additional top-level domain name, the two letter country code, is used routinely to identify countries around the world, for example, ".uk" for United Kingdom, ".ca" for Canada, and ".fr" for France. Because the Internet was created in this country, the two-letter code for the United States, ".us," was not assigned to the original list of top-domain names, though you see it in the URLs of state and local government hosts, including many public schools and community colleges (the latter also use the ".cc" or the ".edu" designations).

In mid-November 2000, the Internet Corporation for Assigned Names and Numbers (ICANN) voted to accept an additional seven new top-level domain suffixes, some of which you may already be seeing:

.aero: restricted use by air transportation industry.

.biz: general use by businesses.

.coop: restricted use by cooperatives.

.info: general use by both commercial and noncommercial sites.

.museum: restricted use by museums.

.name: general use by individuals.

.pro: restricted use by certified professionals and professional entities.

As the Internet grows, you can expect to see the number of top-level domain names grow as well.

Types of Websites

Website authors and sponsors create a variety of pages on the Web. The basic types include: commercial, advocacy, informational, news and journalism, personal, and entertainment. In your efforts to evaluate information quality, the criteria you select will vary according to the type of webpage you encounter.

Commercial Pages. Commercial pages are sponsored by businesses concerned with promoting and selling products. Commercial sites are the largest growing segment on the Web and are identified by the use of the ".com" domain in their URLs. Often they provide reliable information about their products while presenting useful tips in their areas of expertise. For example, manufacturers of carpeting and carpet cleaners are excellent sources for information on how to remove stains. However, do not forget that they are on the Web to make money.

When applying evaluation criteria to commercial pages on the Web, concentrate on examining content. Does the sponsor back up the claims with evidence? Are the claims reasonable and do they sound credible? Does the sponsor provide an opportunity for interactive communication with the public, so that individuals who have tried his product may respond to his promotions?

Advocacy Pages. Advocacy pages are those that exist to influence public opinion. They are found most often under the ".org," ".com," or ".net" domain names. Advocacy pages may be authored by individuals, but usually they are sponsored by organizations dedicated to one or more specific issues. Because they are focused on trying to sell their ideas to the public, advocacy pages are notoriously one-sided. Do not look for them to provide you with information on, or links to, opposing points of view.

This does not mean that advocacy pages have nothing to offer. On the contrary, they are very good sources of information. Their pages are usually heavy on content and contain archives or links to other background materials and articles that support their point of view. Of course, it is up to you to do the digging. Do not forget that you have to look further to get opposing arguments.

When applying evaluation criteria to advocacy pages on the Web, pay close attention to purpose and authority. Who is sponsoring the page, and might they have an ulterior motive? What is their experience and expertise in this field? Look also at content. Are the arguments reasonable and well grounded in known fact? Can they be corroborated?

Informational Pages. Informational pages exist to present factual information. They usually are sponsored by education institutions or government agencies and, not surprisingly, are located most often under the ".edu" or ".gov" domain names. Informational pages strive to maintain objectivity and, when dealing with controversial issues, will usually endeavor to present all sides of an argument.

When applying evaluation criteria to informational pages on the Web, examine authority. Since the name and reputation of the sponsors are closely tied to whatever information is presented on these pages, you need to know who is publishing or underwriting them. When research is presented on the Web, even under the ".gov" and ".edu" domains, it pays to ask just who is funding the research. You might discover that the informational page you are viewing is not quite as objective and unbiased as it appears.

On the Web, advocacy and commercial pages often masquerade as informational pages. How would you characterize, for example, a Pentagon-sponsored website presenting information favorable to the proposed Missile Defense System (MDS)? What would you think about a webpage sponsored by a major timber company that defines clear-cutting as a "best forestry practice"? Even with well-known and respected websites, you should try to determine any hidden motives.

News and Journalism Pages. Sponsored by major media sources (newspapers, television, radio, and magazines), news and journalism pages provide access to current and breaking news, archives of past news stories, online versions of popular journals, and current and archived columns written by reporters and freelance journalists around the world. News and journalism pages are part of the commercial sector and are located under the ".com" domain name.

When applying evaluation criteria to news pages on the Web, pay close attention to currency. This is the area where the Internet has a great advantage over print resources. Major media sources usually update their Web news pages by the hour or even more often. However, they also empty their archives frequently, which can become a problem if you are citing news articles in your research paper. Remember, always make and keep that copy.

With news and journalism pages, you should look at authority and purpose. Are the writers and publishers known for harboring a political bias, for example, a right-wing or far-left philosophy? Do they try to slant or "spin" the news in one direction or another? Of course, the suspected biases of certain news media outlets and individual reporters, whether substantiated or not, are legendary. You will need to corroborate your findings with supporting evidence from other sources.

Personal Pages. Personal pages are published by individuals who may or may not have some kind of affiliation with larger organizations or institutions. Personal pages can, and do, relate to every subject imaginable. They can be serious, informative, humorous, satiric, salacious, or even silly. Their informational content can be accurate and reliable or laced with falsehoods, fabrications, exaggerations, and downright lies.

Personal pages most often are found under the ".com" or ".net" domain names. This is because individuals must purchase server space to host their pages, and this space most often is available through commercial ISPs. Some personal pages can be identified by the use of the tilde (~) near the end of the URL address, indicating the presence of a personal directory on a larger server. Whenever you see the tilde, be aware that the information contained on that page is personal and may or may not represent the position of the sponsoring home site. This is the case with many personal pages created in the ".edu" domain by individual instructors and students at academic institutions.

Many personal pages can be compared to vanity press publications. They contain personal information, résumés, photos, and the like, and often are created for family and friends. However, a growing number have appeared in the past few years with a definite agenda and a political point of view. These pages are not recommended as sources for serious research unless their content can be verified by other reputable sources. Continue to check authority. Do the authors supply credentials to support their points of view? Can you verify these credentials in any way? Do they appear to know their facts, or are they publishing unsubstantiated opinion?

The most recent online status symbol involves purchasing and registering personal domain names. These names can take a multitude of forms, usually a version of an individual's family name, in which case they are easily recognizable. However, some individuals purposely select domain names that point to organizations and agencies with which they have no official connection. On the Web, it always pays to be alert.

Entertainment Pages. Entertainment pages are those that provide humor, games, puzzles, music, drama, or similar activities. Although some entertainment pages are personal pages created by individuals, more are sponsored by commercial interests trying to convince users to buy a particular product or service. They may offer special promotions and provide free, limited access to their software in order to entice users to return and eventually purchase the entire package.

Most entertainment pages carry the ".com" designation in their URLs. When applying evaluation criteria to entertainment pages, look first at the page design. This is a major component of entertainment pages. Poor designs will turn potential buyers or users away, very possibly never to return.

Searching the Web

It is not easy to find exactly what we want on the Web. In order to locate reliable and useful information, we have to sort through tons of irrelevant data, including commercial advertisements and personal pages. And it is not going to get any easier in the future. Every day, with the continuing explosive growth of the Web, we are faced with more pages and more information to sort through.

Today, most of us search the Web by using one of several freely available search tools. Currently, the most popular search tools are search engines, meta-searchers, subject directories, library gateways, and subject-specific databases.

Search Engines

Search engines have been called the card catalogs of the Web. Through their machine-compiled databases, they provide access to a fairly large portion, an estimated 60%, of the publicly available webpages (Lawrence and Giles 1999, p. 107). Search engines use software known as spiders or bots (robots) to crawl from link to link, collecting and indexing the words on millions of webpages.

The words then are fed into huge searchable databases maintained by each engine. Whenever you search the Web using a search engine, you're actually asking the engine to scan its index and match your keywords and phrases with those gathered from the texts of documents scattered across the Internet.

It is important to understand that when you are using a search engine, you are not searching the entire Web. You are searching a portion of the Web captured in a fixed index created at an earlier date. How much earlier is hard to say. Spiders regularly return to the webpages that they index to look for changes. When changes occur, the index is updated to reflect the new information. However, the process of updating depends on how often the spiders make their rounds and then how promptly the information they gather is added to the index. Until a page has been both "spidered" and "indexed," you won't be able to access the new information.

Search engines are nondiscriminatory. They search word by word in the full text of Web documents and return everything they find, making no distinctions concerning content that is serious, outrageous, useful, irrelevant, mundane, or stupid. Enter a keyword into a search engine and it will retrieve a link to every document in which the word appears, even if it appears only once. The sheer number of words indexed by search engines increases the likelihood that they will return hundreds of thousands of irrelevant responses to simple search requests. Everyone who has ever used the Web has experienced the frustration of entering a keyword into a search box and retrieving 100,000 responses, a good share of which are totally unrelated to the subject being searched.

Because they search word by word through many thousands of documents, search engines are very good at finding unique keywords, phrases, quotes, and information buried in webpages. However, when searching for keywords and phrases, don't forget to try more than one search engine. Although software programs may be similar, no two search engines are exactly the same in terms of size, speed, and content; no two search engines use exactly the same ranking schemes, and not every search engine offers you exactly the same search options. Therefore, your search is going to be different on every engine you use. The difference may not be a lot, but it could be significant.

Examples of the largest, most intuitive search engines on the Web today are: Google (http://www.google.com), Alta Vista (http://www.altavista.com), and Fast (http://www.alltheweb.com).

Meta-Searchers

Meta-searchers are the preferred tool of many Web searchers. Meta-searchers search the databases of multiple sets of individual search engines simultaneously. (Always check to make sure they include your favorite engine in their search list). Meta-searchers also provide a quick way of finding out which engines are retrieving the best results for your search. You will see the individual engines referenced in the search results listings.

Examples of some of the more powerful meta-searchers on the Web are: Ixquick (http://www.ixquick.

com), Vivisimo (http://vivisimo.com), and Profusion (http://www.profusion.com).

Subject Directories

Compared to search engines, subject directories are much smaller in size. They are created and maintained by human editors, not electronic spiders or robots. The editors assemble and organize sites into subject categories, but generally they do not engage in extensive review or evaluation of the sites they select.

When you initiate a keyword search of a subject directory's contents, the directory attempts to match your keywords and phrases with those in its written descriptions. Most directories do not compile full-text databases of their own. Instead of storing pages, they point to them. This sometimes creates problems because, once accepted for inclusion in a directory, the webpage could change. The directory might continue to point to a page that has moved or that no longer exists. Dead links are a problem for subject directories, as is a perceived bias toward commercial sites. The most numerous subject directories are general directories, followed by subject-specific databases and library gateways.

General Subject Directories. General subject directories are useful when browsing for information of a more encyclopedic nature or seeking sources of information on popular topics, organizations, commercial sites, and products. Examples of general subject directories are: Yahoo! (http://www.yahoo.com), MSN (http://www.msn.com), AOL (http://www.aol.com), LookSmart (http://www.looksmart.com), Netscape (http://www.netscape.com), Magellan (http://magellan.excite.com), and Open Directory Project (http://dmoz.org).

It is important to note that Web searches may not always be what they seem to be. In the past few years, both subject directories and search engines have been selling rankings in their lists of search results. Website owners pay for having their site listed near the top of the search results. Sometimes the paid listings are identified as "featured" or "partner" sites; sometimes they are called "sponsored links"; sometimes they are not identified at all.

Subject-Specific Directories. Subject-specific databases are devoted to a single subject. They can be created by a host of different sources: professors, researchers, experts, government agencies, commercial interests, and individuals who have a deep interest in or professional knowledge of a particular field and have accumulated information and data about it. Subject-specific databases are useful when searching a narrow topic.

Examples of subject-specific databases are: Search.edu, for college and university sites (http://www.searchedu.com); ERIC Clearinghouses, for education documents (http://www.accesseric.org/index.html); Voice of the Shuttle, for humanities research (http://vos.ucsb.edu); and WebMD, for medical information (http://www.webmd.com).

Library Gateways. Library gateway sites are specialized directories designed to support research and reference needs on the Web and usually are sponsored by large academic and public libraries. Teams of specialists, most often librarians, review, select, and organize pages, by subject, into searchable database collections that point to recommended informational, scholarly, and academic webpages. Many gateway sites provide descriptive annotations of the pages they recommend. Examples of library gateways are: Infomine (http://infomine.ucr.edu), Internet Public Library (http://www.ipl.org), Librarian's Index to the Internet (http://lii.org), Pinakes (http://www.hw.ac.uk/libWWW/irn/pinakes/pinakes.html#about), Argus Clearinghouse (http://www.clearinghouse.net), and the WWW Virtual Library (http://vlib.org/).

In addition to these directories, there are other sources that evaluate websites. Online sources that regularly provide reviews of websites include: Scout Report, by the University of Wisconsin-Madison (http://scout.cs.wisc.edu/report/sr/current/), CIT Infobits, by the University of North Carolina at Chapel Hill (http://www.unc.edu/cit/infobits/index.html), Academe, by the Chronicle of Higher Education Online (http://chronicle.com/free/resources/index.php3), and ResearchBuzz Wire, research news from Moreover.com by Tara Chalishain (http://www.researchbuzz.com/rbuzzwire.html). In addition, an increasing number of print publications in the academic world routinely include websites in their published reviews. Examples are: *Choice Magazine, Library Journal,* and the *Chronicle of Higher Education*.

Conclusion

Every webpage has a point of view. Some websites exist to express the "official" line of their owners. These pages function within organizational or institutional settings where the information is filtered and controlled from the top. The sponsoring organizations may be commercial, educational, military, nonprofit, or professional; but they all share one thing in common: they do not stray far from the market-oriented script that promotes their own interests.

In a separate category, "unofficial" websites exist to provide a way for the individual, who could be anyone from the dissatisfied customer to the whistle-blower, to have his say. The Internet, because of its openness, provides a unique opportunity for the public to access so-called raw information that, due to publishing roadblocks and the excessive costs involved, might otherwise never make it into print. Sometimes, at these unofficial sites, you may obtain information that cannot be found any other way.

To point out that such pages require close scrutiny is probably unnecessary. But their very presence is a gift. It has been said that knowledge is power, and information is the raw material of knowledge. Certainly, those who control the flow of reliable information have access to a large part of the power that comes with knowledge. As long as all sources of information, official and unofficial, continue to be freely available on the Web, every one of us has the opportunity, however small, to share in both the knowledge and the power. That's the beauty of the Internet.

Resources

Electronic

For each of the following Web addresses, the date it was last updated, at the time of the publication of this fastback, is given.

Alexander, Jan, and Tate, Marsha Ann. *Evaluating Web Resources*. Wolfgram Memorial Library, Widener University, July 2001. http://www2.widener.edu/Wolfgram-Memorial-Library/webevaluation/webeval.htm

Barker, Joe. "Evaluating Web Pages: Questions to Ask and Strategies for Getting the Answers." Teaching Library Internet Workshops. University of California, Berkeley, November 2001. http://www.lib.berkeley.edu/TeachingLib/Guides/Internet/EvalQuestions.html

Beck, Susan. "Evaluation Criteria." *The Good, the Bad & the Ugly: Or, Why It's a Good Idea to Evaluate Web Sources*. Institute for Technology-Assisted Learning, New Mexico State University, March 2002. http://lib.nmsu.edu/instruction/evalcrit.html

Beck, Susan E. *Lessons Learned: Exemplary Practices in Teaching Web Evaluation*. New Mexico State University, November 2001. http://lib.nmsu.edu/staff/susabeck/checs98.html

Chamberlain, Ellen. *Bare Bones: A Basic Tutorial on Searching the Web*. University of South Carolina Beaufort, January 2002. http://www.sc.edu/beaufort/library/bones.html

Chamberlain, Ellen, and Mitchell, Miriam. *BCK2SKOL*. University of South Carolina Columbia, October 1999. http://www.sc.edu/bck2skol/

Cramer, Steve. "Evaluating Web Pages." *Guide to Library Research, Part 6: Evaluating Resources*. Duke University Libraries, March 2001. http://www.lib.duke.edu/libguide/evaluating_web.htm

Grassian, Esther. "Thinking Critically About World Wide Web Resources. " *Help Guides*. UCLA College Library. September 2000. http://www.library.ucla.edu/libraries/college/help/critical/index.htm

Harris, Robert. "Evaluating Internet Research Sources." *VirtualSalt*. November 1997. http://www.virtualsalt.com/evalu8it.htm

Henderson, John R. *ICYouSee: T is for Thinking; the ICYouSee Guide to Critical Thinking About What You See on the Web*. Ithaca College Library, October 2001. http://www.ithaca.edu/library/Training/hott.html

Internet Corporation for Assigned Names and Numbers (ICANN). *New TLD Program*. March 2002. http://www.icann.org/tlds/

Kelley, Tina. "Whales in the Minnesota River? Only on the Web, Where Skepticism Is a Required Navigational Aid." *The New York Times Company*, 4 March 1999. http://www.nytimes.com/learning/teachers/featured_articles/19990304thursday.html

Kirk, Elizabeth. *Evaluating Information Found on the Internet*. Sheridan Libraries of the Johns Hopkins University, February 2002. http://www.library.jhu.edu/elp/useit/evaluate/index.html

"Ladies and Gentlemen of the Class of '97: Wear Sunscreen . . ." Article written by Mary Schmich, but falsely attributed to Kurt Vonnegut. June 1997. http://www.wowzone.com/mit97.htm

Ormondroyd, Joan; Engle, Michael; and Cosgrave, Tony. *How to Critically Analyze Information Sources*. Cornell University Library, September 2001. http://www.library.cornell.edu/okuref/research/skill26.htm

Schmich, Mary. "Her Last Web Word Might Be 'Rosewater'." *Chicago Tribune*, 8 August 1997. http://cgi.chicago.tribune.com/news/columnists/schmich/0,1122,SAV-9708080101,00.html

Tillman, Hope. *Evaluating Quality on the Net*. Babson College, May 2000. http://www.hopetillman.com/findqual.html

Print

Alexander, Janet E., and Tate, Marsha Ann. *Web Wisdom: How to Evaluate and Create Information Quality on the Web*. Mahwah, N.J.: Lawrence Erlbaum Associates, 1999.

Harris, Robert. *WebQuester: A Guidebook to the Web*. Guilford, Connecticut: Dushkin, McGraw-Hill, 2000.

Hock, Randolph. *The Extreme Searcher's Guide to Web Search Engines*. 2nd ed. Medford, N.J.: CyberAge Books, Information Today, 2001.

Lawrence, Steve, and Giles, C. Lee. "Accessibility of Information on the Web." *Nature*, 8 July 1999, pp. 107-109.

Order Form

SHIP TO:		
STREET		
CITY/STATE OR PROVINCE/ZIP OR POSTAL CODE		
DAYTIME PHONE NUMBER		PDK MEMBER ROLL NUMBER

QUANTITY	*TITLE*	*PRICE*
	SUBTOTAL	
	Indiana residents add 5% Sales Tax	
	PROCESSING CHARGE	
	TOTAL	

ORDERS MUST INCLUDE PROCESSING CHARGE

Total Merchandise	*Processing Charge*
Up to $50	$5
$50.01 to $100	$10
More than $100	$10 plus 5% of total

Special shipping available upon request.
Prices subject to change without notice.

☐ Payment Enclosed (check payable to Phi Delta Kappa International)

Bill my ☐ VISA ☐ MasterCard ☐ American Express ☐ Discover

ACCT # ________________ DATE ________

EXP DATE __/____ SIGNATURE ________________

Mail or fax your order to: Phi Delta Kappa International, P.O. Box 789, Bloomington, IN 47402-0789. USA
Fax: (812) 339-0018. Phone: (812) 339-1156

For fastest service, phone 1-800-766-1156 and use your credit card.